Music Minus One Trumpet

- ✗ **Bugler's Holiday**
- ✗ **Uplifted**
- ✗ **Battle Hymn / Exodus**
- ✗ **Face It, You've Won**
- ✗ **Melody Of Love**
- ✗ **Morning Sun**
- ✗ **Majestic Melody**
- ✗ **Count On Me**

...the artistry of
David O'Neill

3833

Printed in Canada

COMPACT DISC PAGE AND BAND INFORMATION

MMO CD 3833

Music Minus One

BRASS TRAX
The Trumpet Artistry of David O'Neill

Band No. Complete Version		Band No. Minus Instrument	Page No.
1	Bugler's Holiday	10	4
2	Uplifted	11	8
3	Battle Hymn/Exodus	12	10
4	Face It, You've Won	13	14
5	Melody Of Love	14	18
6	Morning Sun	15	20
7	Majestic Melody	16	22
8	Count On Me	17	26
9	Tuning Notes - A440		

Bugler's Holiday

Music by
LEROY ANDERSON

4

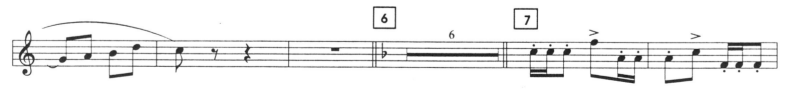

5

6

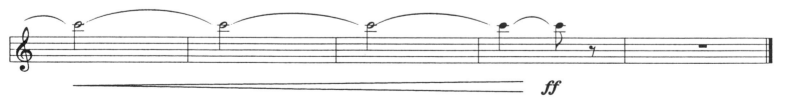

7

Uplifted
(Lift Up The Lord)

Words & Music by
GARY McSPADDEN, BILLEY SMILEY
and SANDI PATTI HELVERING
Arr. by Don Marsh

Battle Hymn/Exodus

Arr. by Don Marsh

This

10

land   is   mine.   God   gave this land to   me.   This   great and

an - cient land   to   me.

Tho I am

just   a man;   when you   are   by   my side,   With the

help of God   I   know I can   be   strong.

ritard

Face It, You've Won

(Face To Faith)

Words & Music by
GARY DRISKELL
Arr. by Don Marsh

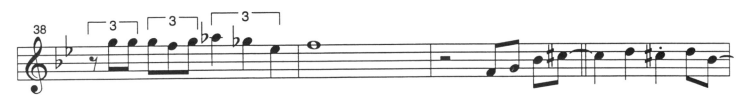

Melody Of Love

Words & Music by
PHILL McHUGH and GREG NELSON
Arr. by Don Marsh

D.S. al Coda

CODA

rit.

Slowly

rit.

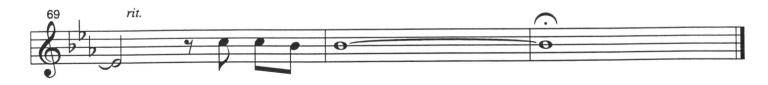

19

Morning Sun

Arr by Don Marsh

†† FACE TO FACE (Breck/Tullar)

mf Gently

†WE WILL SEE HIM AS HE IS (Mark Gersmehl, Scott Douglas)

2nd time to Coda

slight rit.

40

43

D.S. al
Coda

2

48 CODA
scale
scale

53

57

61

64

67

Majestic Melody

Arr. by Don Marsh

HONOR THE LORD (Greg Davis / Greg Fisher)

I SING THE MIGHTY POWER OF GOD (Watts/Gesanbuch der Herzogl)

REJOICE THE LORD IS KING (Wesley / Darwell)

Count On Me

Words and Music by
THOMAS O. CHISHOLM and
WILLIAM M. RUNYAN
Arr by Don Marsh

58

67

74

79

84

91

98

102

108

MMO Compact Disc Catalog

BROADWAY

LES MISERABLES/PHANTOM OF THE OPERA	MMO CD 1016
HITS OF ANDREW LLOYD WEBBER	MMO CD 1054
GUYS AND DOLLS	MMO CD 1067
WEST SIDE STORY 2 CD Set	MMO CD 1100
CABARET 2 CD Set	MMO CD 1110
BROADWAY HEROES AND HEROINES	MMO CD 1121
CAMELOT	MMO CD 1173
BEST OF ANDREW LLOYD WEBBER	MMO CD 1130
THE SOUND OF BROADWAY	MMO CD 1133
BROADWAY MELODIES	MMO CD 1134
BARBRA'S BROADWAY	MMO CD 1144
JEKYLL & HYDE	MMO CD 1151
SHOWBOAT	MMO CD 1160
MY FAIR LADY 2 CD Set	MMO CD 1174
OKLAHOMA	MMO CD 1175
THE SOUND OF MUSIC 2 CD Set	MMO CD 1176
SOUTH PACIFIC	MMO CD 1177
THE KING AND I	MMO CD 1178
FIDDLER ON THE ROOF 2 CD Set	MMO CD 1179
CAROUSEL	MMO CD 1180
PORGY AND BESS	MMO CD 1181
THE MUSIC MAN	MMO CD 1183
ANNIE GET YOUR GUN 2 CD Set	MMO CD 1186
HELLO DOLLY! 2 CD Set	MMO CD 1187
OLIVER 2 CD Set	MMO CD 1189
SUNSET BOULEVARD	MMO CD 1193
GREASE	MMO CD 1196
SMOKEY JOE'S CAFE	MMO CD 1197
MISS SAIGON	MMO CD 1226

CLARINET

MOZART CONCERTO, IN A, K.622	MMO CD 3201
WEBER CONCERTO NO. 1 in Fm. STAMITZ CONC. No. 3 IN Bb	MMO CD 3202
SPOHR CONCERTO NO. 1 in C MINOR OP. 26	MMO CD 3203
WEBER CONCERTO OP. 26, BEETHOVEN TRIO OP. 11	MMO CD 3204
FIRST CHAIR CLARINET SOLOS	MMO CD 3205
THE ART OF THE SOLO CLARINET:	MMO CD 3206
MOZART QUINTET IN A, K.581	MMO CD 3207
BRAHMS SONATAS OP. 120 NO. 1 & 2	MMO CD 3208
WEBER GRAND DUO CONCERTANT WAGNER ADAGIO	MMO CD 3209
SCHUMANN FANTASY OP. 73, 3 ROMANCES OP. 94	MMO CD 3210
EASY CLARINET SOLOS Volume 1 - STUDENT LEVEL	MMO CD 3211
EASY CLARINET SOLOS Volume 2 - STUDENT LEVEL	MMO CD 3212
EASY JAZZ DUETS - STUDENT LEVEL	MMO CD 3213
BEGINNING CONTEST SOLOS - Jerome Bunke, Clinician	MMO CD 3221
BEGINNING CONTEST SOLOS - Harold Wright	MMO CD 3222
INTERMEDIATE CONTEST SOLOS - Stanley Drucker	MMO CD 3223
INTERMEDIATE CONTEST SOLOS - Jerome Bunke, Clinician	MMO CD 3224
ADVANCED CONTEST SOLOS - Stanley Drucker	MMO CD 3225
ADVANCED CONTEST SOLOS - Harold Wright	MMO CD 3226
INTERMEDIATE CONTEST SOLOS - Stanley Drucker	MMO CD 3227
ADVANCED CONTEST SOLOS - Stanley Drucker	MMO CD 3228
ADVANCED CONTEST SOLOS - Harold Wright	MMO CD 3229
BRAHMS Clarinet Quintet in Bm, Op. 115	MMO CD 3230
TEACHER'S PARTNER Basic Clarinet Studies	MMO CD 3231
JEWELS FOR WOODWIND QUINTET	MMO CD 3232
WOODWIND QUINTETS minus CLARINET	MMO CD 3233
FROM DIXIE to SWING	MMO CD 3234
THE VIRTUOSO CLARINETIST Baermann Method, Op. 63 4 CD Set	MMO CD 3240
ART OF THE CLARINET.......... Baermann Method, Op. 64 4 CD Set	MMO CD 3241
POPULAR CONCERT FAVORITES WITH ORCHESTRA	MMO CD 3242
BAND-AIDS CONCERT BAND FAVORITES WITH ORCHESTRA	MMO CD 3243
TWENTY DIXIE CLASSICS	MMO CD 3824
TWENTY RHYTHM BACKGROUNDS TO STANDARDS	MMO CD 3825

PIANO

BEETHOVEN CONCERTO NO. 1 IN C	MMO CD 3001
BEETHOVEN CONCERTO NO. 2 IN Bb	MMO CD 3002
BEETHOVEN CONCERTO NO. 3 IN C MINOR	MMO CD 3003
BEETHOVEN CONCERTO NO. 4 IN G	MMO CD 3004
BEETHOVEN CONCERTO NO. 5 IN Eb (2 CD SET)	MMO CD 3005
GRIEG CONCERTO IN A MINOR OP.16	MMO CD 3006
RACHMANINOFF CONCERTO NO. 2 IN C MINOR	MMO CD 3007
SCHUMANN CONCERTO IN A MINOR	MMO CD 3008
BRAHMS CONCERTO NO. 1 IN D MINOR (2 CD SET)	MMO CD 3009
CHOPIN CONCERTO NO. 1 IN E MINOR OP. 11	MMO CD 3010
MENDELSSOHN CONCERTO NO. 1 IN G MINOR	MMO CD 3011
MOZART CONCERTO NO. 9 IN Eb K.271	MMO CD 3012
MOZART CONCERTO NO. 12 IN A K.414	MMO CD 3013
MOZART CONCERTO NO. 20 IN D MINOR K.466	MMO CD 3014
MOZART CONCERTO NO. 23 IN A K.488	MMO CD 3015
MOZART CONCERTO NO. 24 IN C MINOR K.491	MMO CD 3016

MOZART CONCERTO NO. 26 IN D K.537, CORONATION	MMO CD 3017
MOZART CONCERTO NO. 17 IN G K.453	MMO CD 3018
LISZT CONCERTO NO. 1 IN Eb, WEBER OP. 79	MMO CD 3019
LISZT CONCERTO NO. 2 IN A, HUNGARIAN FANTASIA	MMO CD 3020
J.S. BACH CONCERTO IN F MINOR, J.C. BACH CON. IN Eb	MMO CD 3021
J.S. BACH CONCERTO IN D MINOR	MMO CD 3022
HAYDN CONCERTO IN D	MMO CD 3023
HEART OF THE PIANO CONCERTO	MMO CD 3024
THEMES FROM GREAT PIANO CONCERTI	MMO CD 3025
TSCHAIKOVSKY CONCERTO NO. 1 IN Bb MINOR	MMO CD 3026
ART OF POPULAR PIANO PLAYING, Vol. 1 STUDENT LEVEL	MMO CD 3033
ART OF POPULAR PIANO PLAYING, Vol. 2 STUDENT LEVEL 2 CD Set	MMO CD 3034
'POP' PIANO FOR STARTERS STUDENT LEVEL	MMO CD 3035
DVORAK TRIO IN A MAJOR, OP. 90 "Dumky Trio"	MMO CD 3037
DVORAK QUINTET IN A MAJOR, OP. 81	MMO CD 3038
MENDELSSOHN TRIO IN D MAJOR, OP. 49	MMO CD 3039
MENDELSSOHN TRIO IN C MINOR, OP. 66	MMO CD 3040
BLUES FUSION FOR PIANO	MMO CD 3049
CLAUDE BOLLING SONATA FOR FLUTE AND JAZZ PIANO TRIO	MMO CD 3050
TWENTY DIXIELAND CLASSICS	MMO CD 3051
TWENTY RHYTHM BACKGROUNDS TO STANDARDS	MMO CD 3052
FROM DIXIE to SWING	MMO CD 3053
J.S. BACH BRANDENBURG CONCERTO NO. 5 IN D MAJOR	MMO CD 3054
BACH Cm CONC. for 2 PIANOS / SCHUMANN AND. & VAR., OP. 46 for 2 PIANOS	MMO CD 3055
J.C. BACH Bm CONC. / HAYDN C CONCERTINO / HANDEL CONC. GROSSO in D	MMO CD 3056
J.S. BACH TRIPLE CONCERTO IN A MINOR	MMO CD 3057
FRANCK SYM. VAR. / MENDELSSOHN: CAPRICCO BRILLANT	MMO CD 3058
C.P.E. BACH CONCERTO IN A MINOR	MMO CD 3059

PIANO - FOUR HANDS

RACHMANINOFF Six Scenes ... 4-5th year	MMO CD 3027
ARENSKY 6 Pieces, STRAVINSKY 3 Easy Dances ... 2-3rd year	MMO CD 3028
FAURE: The Dolly Suite	MMO CD 3029
DEBUSSY: Four Pieces	MMO CD 3030
SCHUMANN Pictures from the East ... 4-5th year	MMO CD 3031
BEETHOVEN Three Marches ... 4-5th year	MMO CD 3032
MOZART COMPLETE MUSIC FOR PIANO FOUR HANDS 2 CD Set	MMO CD 3036
MAYKAPAR First Steps, OP. 29 ... 1-2nd year	MMO CD 3041
TSCHAIKOVSKY: 50 Russian Folk Songs	MMO CD 3042
BIZET: 12 Children's Games	MMO CD 3043
GRETCHANINOFF: ON THE GREEN MEADOW	MMO CD 3044
POZZOLI: SMILES OF CHILDHOOD	MMO CD 3045
DIABELLI: PLEASURES OF YOUTH	MMO CD 3046
SCHUBERT: FANTASIA & GRAND SONATA	MMO CD 3047

VIOLIN

BRUCH CONCERTO NO. 1 IN G MINOR OP.26	MMO CD 3100
MENDELSSOHN CONCERTO IN E MINOR	MMO CD 3101
TSCHAIKOVSKY CONCERTO IN D OP. 35	MMO CD 3102
BACH DOUBLE CONCERTO IN D MINOR	MMO CD 3103
BACH CONCERTO IN A MINOR, CONCERTO IN E	MMO CD 3104
BACH BRANDENBURG CONCERTI NOS. 4 & 5	MMO CD 3105
BACH BRANDENBURG CONCERTO NO. 2,TRIPLE CONCERTO	MMO CD 3106
BACH CONCERTO IN DM, (FROM CONCERTO FOR HARPSICHORD)	MMO CD 3107
BRAHMS CONCERTO IN D OP. 77	MMO CD 3108
CHAUSSON POEME, SCHUBERT RONDO	MMO CD 3109
LALO SYMPHONIE ESPAGNOLE	MMO CD 3110
MOZART CONCERTO IN D K.218, VIVALDI CON. AM OP. 3 NO. 6	MMO CD 3111
MOZART CONCERTO IN A K.219	MMO CD 3112
WIENIAWSKI CON. IN D. SARASATE ZIGEUNERWEISEN	MMO CD 3113
VIOTTI CONCERTO NO. 22 IN A MINOR	MMO CD 3114
BEETHOVEN 2 ROMANCES, SONATA NO. 5 IN F "SPRING SONATA"	MMO CD 3115
SAINT-SAENS INTRODUCTION & RONDO, MOZART SERENADE K. 204, ADAGIO K.261	MMO CD 3116
BEETHOVEN CONCERTO IN D OP. 61(2 CD SET)	MMO CD 3117
THE CONCERTMASTER - Orchestral Excerpts	MMO CD 3118
AIR ON A G STRING Favorite Encores with Orchestra Easy Medium	MMO CD 3119
CONCERT PIECES FOR THE SERIOUS VIOLINIST Easy Medium	MMO CD 3120
18TH CENTURY VIOLIN PIECES	MMO CD 3121
ORCHESTRAL FAVORITES - Volume 1 - Easy Level	MMO CD 3122
ORCHESTRAL FAVORITES - Volume 2 - Medium Level	MMO CD 3123
ORCHESTRAL FAVORITES - Volume 3 - Med to Difficult Level	MMO CD 3124
THE THREE B'S BACH/BEETHOVEN/BRAHMS	MMO CD 3125
VIVALDI Concerto in A Minor Op. 3 No. 6. in D Op. 3 No. 9. Double Concerto Op. 3 No. 8	MMO CD 3126
VIVALDI-THE FOUR SEASONS (2 CD Set)	MMO CD 3127
VIVALDI Concerto in Eb, Op. 8, No. 5. ALBINONI Concerto in A	MMO CD 3128
VIVALDI Concerto in E, Op. 3, No. 12. Concerto in C Op. 8, No. 6 "Il Piacere"	MMO CD 3129
SCHUBERT Three Sonatinas	MMO CD 3130
HAYDN String Quartet Op. 76 No. 1	MMO CD 3131
HAYDN String Quartet Op. 76 No. 2	MMO CD 3132
HAYDN String Quartet Op. 76 No. 3 "Emperor"	MMO CD 3133
HAYDN String Quartet Op. 76 No. 4 "Sunrise"	MMO CD 3134
HAYDN String Quartet Op. 76 No. 5	MMO CD 3135

MMO Music Group, 50 Executive Boulevard, Elmsford, New York 10523, 1 (800) 669-7464

6/6/97 PSG

MMO Compact Disc Catalog

HAYDN String Quartet Op. 76 No. 6 ....MMO CD 3136
BEAUTIFUL MUSIC FOR TWO VIOLINS 1st position, vol. 1 ....MMO CD 3137 ★
BEAUTIFUL MUSIC FOR TWO VIOLINS 2nd position, vol. 2 ....MMO CD 3138 ★
BEAUTIFUL MUSIC FOR TWO VIOLINS 3rd position, vol. 3 ....MMO CD 3139 ★
BEAUTIFUL MUSIC FOR TWO VIOLINS 1st, 2nd, 3rd position, vol. 4 ....MMO CD 3140 ★
TEACHER'S PARTNER Basic Violin Studies 1st year ....MMO CD 3142
DVORAK STRING TRIO "Terzetto", OP. 74 2 violins/viola ....MMO CD 3143
SIBELIUS VIOLIN Concerto in D Minor, OPUS 47 ....MMO CD 3144

★Lovely folk tunes and selections from the classics, chosen for their melodic beauty and technical value.
They have been skillfully transcribed and edited by Samuel Applebaum, one of America's foremost teachers.

GUITAR

BOCCHERINI Quintet No. 4 in D "Fandango" ....MMO CD 3601
GIULIANI Quintet in A Op. 65 ....MMO CD 3602
CLASSICAL GUITAR DUETS ....MMO CD 3603
RENAISSANCE & BAROQUE GUITAR DUETS ....MMO CD 3604
CLASSICAL & ROMANTIC GUITAR DUETS ....MMO CD 3605
GUITAR AND FLUTE DUETS Volume 1 ....MMO CD 3606
GUITAR AND FLUTE DUETS Volume 2 ....MMO CD 3607
BLUEGRASS GUITAR ....MMO CD 3608
GEORGE BARNES GUITAR METHOD Lessons from a Master ....MMO CD 3609
HOW TO PLAY FOLK GUITAR 2 CD Set ....MMO CD 3610
FAVORITE FOLKS SONGS FOR GUITAR ....MMO CD 3611
FOR GUITARS ONLY! Jimmy Raney Small Band Arrangements ....MMO CD 3612
TEN DUETS FOR TWO GUITARS Geo. Barnes/Carl Kress ....MMO CD 3613
PLAY THE BLUES GUITAR A Dick Weissman Method ....MMO CD 3614
ORCHESTRAL GEMS FOR CLASSICAL GUITAR ....MMO CD 3615

FLUTE

MOZART Concerto No. 2 in D, QUANTZ Concerto in G ....MMO CD 3300
MOZART Concerto in G K.313 ....MMO CD 3301
BACH Suite No. 2 in B Minor ....MMO CD 3302
BOCCHERINI Concerto in D, VIVALDI Concerto in G Minor "La Notte",
MOZART Andante for Strings ....MMO CD 3303
HAYDN Divertimento, VIVALDI Concerto in D Op. 10 No. 3 "Bullfinch",
FREDERICK THE GREAT Concerto in C ....MMO CD 3304
VIVALDI Conc. in F; TELEMANN Conc. in D; LECLAIR Conc. in C ....MMO CD 3305
BACH Brandenburg No. 2 in F, HAYDN Concerto in D ....MMO CD 3306
BACH Triple Concerto, VIVALDI Concerto in D Minor ....MMO CD 3307
MOZART Quartet in F, STAMITZ Quartet in F ....MMO CD 3308
HAYDN 4 London Trios for 2 Flutes & Cello ....MMO CD 3309
BACH Brandenburg Concerti Nos. 4 & 5 ....MMO CD 3310
MOZART 3 Flute Quartets in D, A and C ....MMO CD 3311
TELEMANN Suite in A Minor, GLUCK Scene from 'Orpheus',
PERGOLESI Concerto in G (2 CD Set) ....MMO CD 3312
FLUTE SONG: Easy Familiar Classics ....MMO CD 3313
VIVALDI Concerti in D, G, and F ....MMO CD 3314
VIVALDI Concerti in A Minor, G, and D ....MMO CD 3315
EASY FLUTE SOLOS Beginning Students Volume 1 ....MMO CD 3316
EASY FLUTE SOLOS Beginning Students Volume 2 ....MMO CD 3317
EASY JAZZ DUETS Student Level ....MMO CD 3318
FLUTE & GUITAR DUETS Volume 1 ....MMO CD 3319
FLUTE & GUITAR DUETS Volume 2 ....MMO CD 3320
BEGINNING CONTEST SOLOS Murray Panitz ....MMO CD 3321
BEGINNING CONTEST SOLOS Donald Peck ....MMO CD 3322
INTERMEDIATE CONTEST SOLOS Julius Baker ....MMO CD 3323
INTERMEDIATE CONTEST SOLOS Donald Peck ....MMO CD 3324
ADVANCED CONTEST SOLOS Murray Panitz ....MMO CD 3325
ADVANCED CONTEST SOLOS Julius Baker ....MMO CD 3326
INTERMEDIATE CONTEST SOLOS Donald Peck ....MMO CD 3327
ADVANCED CONTEST SOLOS Murray Panitz ....MMO CD 3328
ADVANCED CONTEST SOLOS Julius Baker ....MMO CD 3329
BEGINNING CONTEST SOLOS Doriot Anthony Dwyer ....MMO CD 3330
INTERMEDIATE CONTEST SOLOS Doriot Anthony Dwyer ....MMO CD 3331
ADVANCED CONTEST SOLOS Doriot Anthony Dwyer ....MMO CD 3332
FIRST CHAIR SOLOS with Orchestral Accompaniment ....MMO CD 3333
TEACHER'S PARTNER Basic Flute Studies 1st year ....MMO CD 3334
THE JOY OF WOODWIND MUSIC ....MMO CD 3335
JEWELS FOR WOODWIND QUINTET ....MMO CD 3336
BOLLING: SUITE FOR FLUTE/JAZZ PIANO TRIO ....MMO CD 3342
HANDEL / TELEMANN SIX SONATAS 2 CD Set ....MMO CD 3343
BACH SONATA NO. 1 in Bm / KUHLAU TWO DUETS in Em/D MAJOR 2 CD Set ....MMO CD 3344
KUHLAU TRIO for 3 FLUTES in Eb, OP. 86 / BACH 2 SONATAS IN Eb/A 2 CD Set ..MMO CD 3345
PEPUSCH SONATA IN C / TELEMANN SONATA IN Cm ....MMO CD 3346
QUANTZ TRIO SONATA IN Cm / BACH GIGUE / ABEL SON. 2 IN F ....MMO CD 3347
TELEMANN CONCERTO NO. 1 in D / CORRETTE SONATA IN E MINOR ....MMO CD 3348
TELEMANN TRIO IN F / Bb MAJOR / HANDEL SON. #3 IN C MAJOR ....MMO CD 3349
MARCELLO / TELEMANN / HANDEL SONATAS IN F MAJOR ....MMO CD 3350
CONCERT BAND FAVORITES WITH ORCHESTRA ....MMO CD 3351
BAND-AIDS CONCERT BAND FAVORITES WITH ORCHESTRA ....MMO CD 3352

RECORDER

PLAYING THE RECORDER Folk Songs of Many Naitons ....MMO CD 3337
LET'S PLAY THE RECORDER Beginning Children's Method ....MMO CD 3338
YOU CAN PLAY THE RECORDER Beginning Adult Method ....MMO CD 3339
3 SONATAS FOR FLUTE, HARPSICHORD & VIOLA DA GAMBA ....MMO CD 3340
3 SONATAS FOR ALTO RECORDER ....MMO CD 3341

FRENCH HORN

MOZART Concerti No. 2 & No. 3 in Eb. K. 417 & 447 ....MMO CD 3501
BAROQUE BRASS AND BEYOND ....MMO CD 3502
MUSIC FOR BRASS ENSEMBLE ....MMO CD 3503
MOZART Sonatas for Two Horns ....MMO CD 3504
BEGINNING CONTEST SOLOS Mason Jones ....MMO CD 3511
BEGINNING CONTEST SOLOS Myron Bloom ....MMO CD 3512
INTERMEDIATE CONTEST SOLOS Dale Clevenger ....MMO CD 3513
INTERMEDIATE CONTEST SOLOS Mason Jones ....MMO CD 3514
ADVANCED CONTEST SOLOS Myron Bloom ....MMO CD 3515
ADVANCED CONTEST SOLOS Dale Clevenger ....MMO CD 3516
INTERMEDIATE CONTEST SOLOS Mason Jones ....MMO CD 3517
ADVANCED CONTEST SOLOS Myron Bloom ....MMO CD 3518
INTERMEDIATE CONTEST SOLOS Dale Clevenger ....MMO CD 3519
FRENCH HORN WOODWIND MUSIC ....MMO CD 3520
MASTERPIECES FOR WOODWIND QUINTET ....MMO CD 3521
FRENCH HORN UP FRONT BRASS QUINTETS ....MMO CD 3522
HORN OF PLENTY BRASS QUINTETS ....MMO CD 3523
BAND-AIDS CONCERT BAND FAVORITES WITH ORCHESTRA ....MMO CD 3524

TRUMPET

THREE CONCERTI: HAYDN, TELEMANN, FASCH ....MMO CD 3801
TRUMPET SOLOS Student Level Volume 1 ....MMO CD 3802
TRUMPET SOLOS Student Level Volume 2 ....MMO CD 3803
EASY JAZZ DUETS Student Level ....MMO CD 3804
MUSIC FOR BRASS ENSEMBLE Brass Quintets ....MMO CD 3805
FIRST CHAIR TRUMPET SOLOS with Orchestral Accompaniment ....MMO CD 3806
THE ART OF THE SOLO TRUMPET with Orchestral Accompaniment ....MMO CD 3807
BAROQUE BRASS AND BEYOND Brass Quintets ....MMO CD 3808
THE COMPLETE ARBAN DUETS all of the classic studies ....MMO CD 3809
SOUSA MARCHES PLUS BEETHOVEN, BERLIOZ, STRAUSS ....MMO CD 3810
BEGINNING CONTEST SOLOS Gerard Schwarz ....MMO CD 3811
BEGINNING CONTEST SOLOS Armando Ghitalla ....MMO CD 3812
INTERMEDIATE CONTEST SOLOS Robert Nagel, Soloist ....MMO CD 3813
INTERMEDIATE CONTEST SOLOS Gerard Schwarz ....MMO CD 3814
ADVANCED CONTEST SOLOS Robert Nagel, Soloist ....MMO CD 3815
CONTEST SOLOS Armando Ghitalla ....MMO CD 3816
INTERMEDIATE CONTEST SOLOS Gerard Schwarz ....MMO CD 3817
ADVANCED CONTEST SOLOS Robert Nagel, Soloist ....MMO CD 3818
ADVANCED CONTEST SOLOS Armando Ghilalla ....MMO CD 3819
BEGINNING CONTEST SOLOS Raymond Crisara ....MMO CD 3820
BEGINNING CONTEST SOLOS Raymond Crisara ....MMO CD 3821
INTERMEDIATE CONTEST SOLOS Raymond Crisara ....MMO CD 3822
TEACHER'S PARTNER Basic Trumpet Studies 1st year ....MMO CD 3823
TWENTY DIXIELAND CLASSICS ....MMO CD 3824
TWENTY RHYTHM BACKGROUNDS TO STANDARDS ....MMO CD 3825
FROM DIXIE TO SWING ....MMO CD 3826
TRUMPET PIECES BRASS QUINTETS ....MMO CD 3827
MODERN BRASS QUINTETS ....MMO CD 3828
WHEN JAZZ WAS YOUNG The Bob Wilber All Stars ....MMO CD 3829
CONCERT BAND FAVORITES WITH ORCHESTRA ....MMO CD 3831
BAND-AIDS CONCERT BAND FAVORITES WITH ORCHESTRA ....MMO CD 3832

TROMBONE

TROMBONE SOLOS Student Level Volume 1 ....MMO CD 3901
TROMBONE SOLOS Student Level Volume 2 ....MMO CD 3902
EASY JAZZ DUETS Student Level ....MMO CD 3903
BAROQUE BRASS & BEYOND Brass Quintets ....MMO CD 3904
MUSIC FOR BRASS ENSEMBLE Brass Quintets ....MMO CD 3905
BEGINNING CONTEST SOLOS Per Brevig ....MMO CD 3911
BEGINNING CONTEST SOLOS Jay Friedman ....MMO CD 3912
INTERMEDIATE CONTEST SOLOS Keith Brown, Professor, Indiana University...MMO CD 3913
INTERMEDIATE CONTEST SOLOS Jay Friedman ....MMO CD 3914
ADVANCED CONTEST SOLOS Keith Brown, Professor, Indiana University ......MMO CD 3915
ADVANCED CONTEST SOLOS Per Brevig ....MMO CD 3916
ADVANCED CONTEST SOLOS Keith Brown, Professor, Indiana University ......MMO CD 3917
ADVANCED CONTEST SOLOS Jay Friedman ....MMO CD 3918
ADVANCED CONTEST SOLOS Per Brevig ....MMO CD 3919
TEACHER'S PARTNER Basic Trombone Studies 1st year ....MMO CD 3920
TWENTY DIXIELAND CLASSICS ....MMO CD 3924
TWENTY RHYTHM BACKGROUNDS TO STANDARDS ....MMO CD 3925
FROM DIXIE TO SWING ....MMO CD 3926
STICKS & BONES BRASS QUINTETS ....MMO CD 3927
FOR TROMBONES ONLY MORE BRASS QUINTETS ....MMO CD 3928
POPULAR CONCERT FAVORITES The Stuttgart Festival Band ....MMO CD 3929
BAND-AIDS CONCERT BAND FAVORITES WITH ORCHESTRA ....MMO CD 3930

MMO Music Group, 50 Executive Boulevard, Elmsford, New York 10523, 1 (800) 669-7464

6/6/97 PSG

MMO Compact Disc Catalog

TENOR SAXOPHONE

TENOR SAXOPHONE SOLOS Student Edition Volume 1	MMO CD 4201
TENOR SAXOPHONE SOLOS Student Edition Volume 2	MMO CD 4202
EASY JAZZ DUETS FOR TENOR SAXOPHONE	MMO CD 4203
FOR SAXES ONLY Arranged by Bob Wilber	MMO CD 4204
BLUES FUSION	MMO CD 4205
JOBIM BRAZILIAN BOSSA NOVAS with STRINGS	MMO CD 4206
TWENTY DIXIE CLASSICS	MMO CD 4207
TWENTY RHYTHM BACKGROUNDS TO STANDARDS	MMO CD 4208
PLAY LEAD IN A SAX SECTION	MMO CD 4209
DAYS OF WINE & ROSES Sax Section Minus You	MMO CD 4210
FRENCH & AMERICAN SAXOPHONE QUARTETS	MMO CD 4211
CONCERT BAND FAVORITES WITH ORCHESTRA	MMO CD 4212
BAND AIDS CONCERT BAND FAVORITES	MMO CD 4213
THE ART OF IMPROVISATION, VOL. 1	MMO CD 7005
THE ART OF IMPROVISATION, VOL. 2	MMO CD 7006
THE BLUES MINUS YOU/MAL WALDRON	MMO CD 7007
TAKE A CHORUS/J. RANEY/STAN GETZ	MMO CD 7008

CELLO

DVORAK Concerto in B Minor Op. 104 (2 CD Set)	MMO CD 3701
C.P.E. BACH Concerto in A Minor	MMO CD 3702
BOCCHERINI Concerto in Bb, BRUCH Kol Nidrei	MMO CD 3703
TEN PIECES FOR CELLO	MMO CD 3704
SCHUMANN Concerto in Am & Other Selections	MMO CD 3705
CLAUDE BOLLING Suite For Cello & Jazz Piano Trio	MMO CD 3706

OBOE

ALBINONI Concerti in Bb, Op. 7 No. 3, No. 6, D. Op. 9 No. 2 in Dm	MMO CD 3400
TELEMANN Conc. in Fm; HANDEL Conc. in Bb; VIVALDI Conc.in Dm	MMO CD 3401
MOZART Quartet in F K.370, STAMITZ Quartet in F Op. 8 No. 3	MMO CD 3402
BACH Brandenburg Concerto No. 2, Telemann Con. in Am	MMO CD 3403
CLASSIC SOLOS FOR OBOE Delia Montenegro, Soloist	MMO CD 3404
MASTERPIECES FOR WOODWIND QUINTET	MMO CD 3405
THE JOY OF WOODWIND QUINTETS	MMO CD 3406
PEPUSCH SONATAS IN C/TELEMANN SONATA IN Cm	MMO CD 3407
QUANTZ TRIO SONATA IN Cm/BACH GIGUE/ABEL SONATAS IN F	MMO CD 3408

ALTO SAXOPHONE

ALTO SAXOPHONE SOLOS Student Edition Volume 1	MMO CD 4101
ALTO SAXOPHONE SOLOS Student Edition Volume 2.	MMO CD 4102
EASY JAZZ DUETS FOR ALTO SAXOPHONE	MMO CD 4103
FOR SAXES ONLY Arranged Bob Wilber	MMO CD 4104
TEACHER'S PARTNER Basic Alto Sax Studies 1st year	MMO CD 4105
JOBIM BRAZILIAN BOSSA NOVAS with STRINGS	MMO CD 4106
BEGINNING CONTEST SOLOS Paul Brodie, Canadian Soloist	MMO CD 4111
BEGINNING CONTEST SOLOS Vincent Abato	MMO CD 4112
INTERMEDIATE CONTEST SOLOS Paul Brodie, Canadian Soloist	MMO CD 4113
INTERMEDIATE CONTEST SOLOS Vincent Abato	MMO CD 4114
ADVANCED CONTEST SOLOS Paul Brodie. Canadian Soloist	MMO CD 4115
ADVANCED CONTEST SOLOS Vincent Abato	MMO CD 4116
ADVANCED CONTEST SOLOS Paul Brodie, Canadian Soloist	MMO CD 4117
ADVANCED CONTEST SOLOS Vincent Abato	MMO CD 4118
PLAY LEAD IN A SAX SECTION	MMO CD 4120
DAYS OF WINE & ROSES/SENSUAL SAX	MMO CD 4121
TWENTY DIXIELAND CLASSICS	MMO CD 4124
TWENTY RHYTHM BACKGROUNDS TO STANDARDS	MMO CD 4125
CONCERT BAND FAVORITES WITH ORCHESTRA	MMO CD 4126
BAND AIDS CONCERT BAND FAVORITES	MMO CD 4127
FRENCH & AMERICAN SAXOPHONE QUARTETS	MMO CD 4128
BLUES FUSION FOR SAXOPHONE	MMO CD 4205
THE ART OF IMPROVISATION, VOL. 1	MMO CD 7005
THE ART OF IMPROVISATION, VOL. 2	MMO CD 7006
THE BLUES MINUS YOU/MAL WALDRON	MMO CD 7007
TAKE A CHORUS/J. RANEY/STAN GETZ	MMO CD 7008

SOPRANO SAXOPHONE

FRENCH & AMERICAN SAXOPHONE QUARTETS	MMO CD 4801

BARITONE SAXOPHONE

FRENCH & AMERICAN SAXOPHONE QUARTETS	MMO CD 4901

VOCAL

SCHUBERT GERMAN LIEDER - High Voice, Volume 1	MMO CD 4001
SCHUBERT GERMAN LIEDER - Low Voice, Volume 1	MMO CD 4002
SCHUBERT GERMAN LIEDER - High Voice, Volume 2	MMO CD 4003
SCHUBERT GERMAN LIEDER - Low Voice, Volume 2	MMO CD 4004
BRAHMS GERMAN LIEDER - High Voice	MMO CD 4005
BRAHMS GERMAN LIEDER - Low Voice	MMO CD 4006
EVERYBODY'S FAVORITE SONGS - High Voice, Volume 1	MMO CD 4007
EVERYBODY'S FAVORITE SONGS - Low Voice, Volume 1	MMO CD 4008
EVERYBODY'S FAVORITE SONGS - High Voice, Volume 2	MMO CD 4009
EVERYBODY'S FAVORITE SONGS - Low Voice, Volume 2	MMO CD 4010
17th/18th CENT. ITALIAN SONGS - High Voice, Volume 1	MMO CD 4011
17th/18th CENT. ITALIAN SONGS - Low Voice, Volume 1	MMO CD 4012

17th/18th CENT. ITALIAN SONGS - High Voice, Volume 2	MMO CD 4013
17th/18th CENT. ITALIAN SONGS - Low Voice, Volume 2	MMO CD 4014
FAMOUS SOPRANO ARIAS	MMO CD 4015
FAMOUS MEZZO-SOPRANO ARIAS	MMO CD 4016
FAMOUS TENOR ARIAS	MMO CD 4017
FAMOUS BARITONE ARIAS	MMO CD 4018
FAMOUS BASS ARIAS	MMO CD 4019
WOLF GERMAN LIEDER FOR HIGH VOICE	MMO CD 4020
WOLF GERMAN LIEDER FOR LOW VOICE	MMO CD 4021
STRAUSS GERMAN LIEDER FOR HIGH VOICE	MMO CD 4022
STRAUSS GERMAN LIEDER FOR LOW VOICE	MMO CD 4023
SCHUMANN GERMAN LIEDER FOR HIGH VOICE	MMO CD 4024
SCHUMANN GERMAN LIEDER FOR LOW VOICE	MMO CD 4025
MOZART ARIAS FOR SOPRANO	MMO CD 4026
VERDI ARIAS FOR SOPRANO	MMO CD 4027
ITALIAN ARIAS FOR SOPRANO	MMO CD 4028
FRENCH ARIAS FOR SOPRANO	MMO CD 4029
ORATORIO ARIAS FOR SOPRANO	MMO CD 4030
ORATORIO ARIAS FOR ALTO	MMO CD 4031
ORATORIO ARIAS FOR TENOR	MMO CD 4032
ORATORIO ARIAS FOR BASS	MMO CD 4033
BEGINNING SOPRANO SOLOS Kate Hurney	MMO CD 4041
INTERMEDIATE SOPRANO SOLOS Kate Hurney	MMO CD 4042
BEGINNING MEZZO SOPRANO SOLOS Fay Kittelson	MMO CD 4043
INTERMEDIATE MEZZO SOPRANO SOLOS Fay Kittelson	MMO CD 4044
ADVANCED MEZZO SOPRANO SOLOS Fay Kittelson	MMO CD 4045
BEGINNING CONTRALTO SOLOS Carline Ray	MMO CD 4046
BEGINNING TENOR SOLOS George Shirley	MMO CD 4047
INTERMEDIATE TENOR SOLOS George Shirley	MMO CD 4048
ADVANCED TENOR SOLOS George Shirley	MMO CD 4049

DOUBLE BASS

BEGINNING TO INTERMEDIATE CONTEST SOLOS David Walter	MMO CD 4301
INTERMEDIATE TO ADVANCED CONTEST SOLOS David Walter	MMO CD 4302
FOR BASSISTS ONLY Ken Smith, Soloist	MMO CD 4303
THE BEAT GOES ON Jazz - Funk, Latin, Pop-Rock	MMO CD 4304
FROM DIXIE TO SWING	MMO CD 4305

DRUMS

MODERN JAZZ DRUMMING 2 CD Set	MMO CD 5001
FOR DRUMMERS ONLY	MMO CD 5002
WIPE OUT	MMO CD 5003
SIT-IN WITH JIM CHAPIN	MMO CD 5004
DRUM STAR Trios/Quartets/Quintets Minus You	MMO CD 5005
DRUMPADSTICKSKIN Jazz play-alongs with small groups	MMO CD 5006
CLASSICAL PERCUSSION 2 CD Set	MMO CD 5009
EIGHT MEN IN SEARCH OF A DRUMMER	MMO CD 5010
FROM DIXIE TO SWING	MMO CD 5011
FABULOUS SOUNDS OF ROCK DRUMS	MMO CD 5012

VIOLA

VIOLA SOLOS with piano accompaniment	MMO CD 4501
DVORAK STRING TRIO "Terzetto", OP. 74 2 Vins/Viola	MMO CD 4503

VIBES

FOR VIBISTS ONLY	MMO CD 5101
GOOD VIB-RATIONS	MMO CD 5102

BASSOON

SOLOS FOR THE BASSOON Janet Grice, Soloist	MMO CD 4601
MASTERPIECES FOR WOODWIND MUSIC	MMO CD 4602
THE JOY OF WOODWIND QUINTETS	MMO CD 4603

BANJO

BLUEGRASS BANJO Classic & Favorite Banjo Pieces	MMO CD 4401
PLAY THE FIVE STRING BANJO Vol. 1 Dick Weissman Method	MMO CD 4402
PLAY THE FIVE STRING BANJO Vol. 2 Dick Weissman Method	MMO CD 4403

TUBA or BASS TROMBONE

HE'S NOT HEAVY, HE'S MY TUBA	MMO CD 4701
SWEETS FOR BRASS	MMO CD 4702

INSTRUCTIONAL METHODS

RUTGERS UNIVERSITY MUSIC DICTATION/EAR TRAINING COURSE (7 CD Set)	MMO CD 7001
EVOLUTION OF THE BLUES	MMO CD 7004
THE ART OF IMPROVISATION, VOL. 1	MMO CD 7005
THE ART OF IMPROVISATION, VOL. 2	MMO CD 7006
THE BLUES MINUS YOU Ed Xiques, Soloist	MMO CD 7007
TAKE A CHORUS minus Bb/Eb Instruments	MMO CD 7008
UNDERSTANDING JAZZ	MMO CD 7009

MMO Music Group, 50 Executive Boulevard, Elmsford, New York 10523, 1 (800) 669-7464

Music Minus One Trumpet

- ✗ **Bugler's Holiday**
- ✗ **Uplifted**
- ✗ **Battle Hymn / Exodus**
- ✗ **Face It, You've Won**
- ✗ **Melody Of Love**
- ✗ **Morning Sun**
- ✗ **Majestic Melody**
- ✗ **Count On Me**

...the artistry of
David O'Neill

3833

MMO Music Group, 50 Executive Boulevard, Elmsford, New York 10523, 1 (800) 669-7464